Take a trip to
SOUTH
KOREA

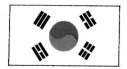

Keith Lye

General Editor
Henry Pluckrose

Franklin Watts

London   New York   Sydney   Toronto

Facts about South Korea

Area:
98,484 sq. km.
(38,025 sq. miles)

Population:
39,331,000

Capital:
Seoul

Largest cities:
Seoul (8,367,000)
Pusan (3,160,000)
Taegu (1,607,000)
In'chon (1,085,000)

Official language:
Korean

Religions:
Buddhism, Christianity,
Confucianism

Main exports:
Textiles, manufactured
goods, chemicals

Currency:
Won

Franklin Watts Limited
12a Golden Square
London W1

ISBN: UK Edition 0 86313 271 5
ISBN: US Edition 0 531 10012 X
Library of Congress Catalog
Card No: 85–50164

© Franklin Watts Limited 1985

Typeset by Ace Filmsetting Ltd,
Frome, Somerset
Printed in Hong Kong

Maps: Tony Payne
Design: Edward Kinsey
Stamps: Stanley Gibbons Limited
Photographs: Korea National
Tourism Corporation; Robert Harding,
4, 5, 6, 7, 13, 14, 15, 26, 27; Paul
Forrester, 8; Zefa, 3, 11, 12, 31
Front cover: Zefa
Back cover: Korea National Tourism
Corporation

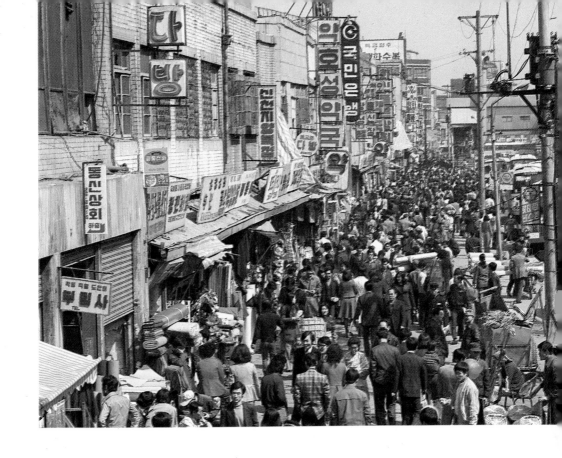

South Korea, officially called the Republic of Korea, is the southern part of a finger-like area of land, named the Korean peninsula. To the north is the separate country of North Korea, which is joined to China and Russia. This street is in South Korea's capital, Seoul.

South Koreans resemble the Chinese and Japanese. About one-third of the people work on farms. Summers are warm, with average July temperatures of 25°C (77°F). The average rainfall is 1,250 mm (49 inches) a year.

Most of the rain comes in June to October. But snow often covers the land in winter. The average temperatures in January are $-3°C$ ($27°F$). The south coast is warmer.

South Korea is a land of beautiful mountains and fertile plains. The people call the country Choson, which means the Land of Morning Calm. The country's highest peak, Halla-san, is on the island of Cheju Do.

South Korea has a long coastline. The west coast facing the Yellow Sea and the south coast are jagged, with many small offshore islands. The east coast, shown here, is smoother. It faces the Sea of Japan.

The picture shows some stamps and money used in South Korea. The main unit of currency is the won, which contains 100 jeon.

WORLD MAP

Korea

CHINA

U.S.S.R.

▲ *Paektu-san*

• Ch'ŏngjin

NORTH KOREA

Yalu

Hamhŭng

• Hŭngnam

P'yŏngyang

Cease Fire Line

Panmunjom

SEA OF JAPAN

• Seoul

Inch'ŏn

REPUBLIC OF **KOREA**

YELLOW SEA

Taejŏn

Taegu

• Kyŏngju

• Ulsan

Masan

Kwangju •

• Pusan

JAPAN

Cheju Do

▲ *Halla-san*

9

Panmunjom is on the frontier between North and South Korea. Here, a treaty was signed in 1953, ending a war between the Communist North, whose capital is P'yongyang, and the non-Communist South. Soldiers from North and South patrol the frontier.

Seoul, South Korea's capital, is in the northwest, not far from the border with North Korea. The city, along with the rest of the country, suffered greatly during the Korean War (1950–53). It is now a busy modern city and one of the world's 20 largest cities.

Pusan is the second largest city. It is on the southeastern coast and is the country's main seaport. It exports fish, farm products and manufactured goods from its many factories. About three out of every five South Koreans live in cities and towns.

Military service is compulsory in South Korea and soldiers, sailors and airmen appear in parades on Armed Forces Day. South Korea is a republic. It is ruled by the President, a State Council of Ministers and an elected National Assembly.

At harvest time, all members of the family work together to bring in the crops. Here, the farmers are threshing the grain. Most farms in South Korea are small and family-owned.

Many Korean farmers use simple tools, such as animal-drawn ploughs. Cropland covers about one-fifth of the country. The main crops are rice, other grains, beans and tobacco.

Red peppers are dried in the sun.
Peppers are widely grown, because
the people enjoy spicy food.
Farmhouses with thatched roofs and
clay walls are common sights in
South Korea.

Farmers go to market to buy and sell cattle. Animal farming is important. South Korean farmers own a total of more than 1.5 million cattle, 2 million pigs and 46 million poultry.

Cars are one of South Korea's many industrial products. Until recently, most factories made household goods and the country is one of the world's leading makers of television sets and radios. Many heavy industries are now being set up.

South Korea's heavy industries include large steel works, such as this one at Pohang in the southeast, shipbuilding and chemical plants. The most important mineral produced in South Korea is tungsten. This metal is used in the steel, electrical and machine tool industries.

Beautiful cotton and silk fabrics are manufactured. Women often wear short jackets and long skirts, while older men wear loose white coats and baggy trousers. But many young people prefer western clothes.

The arts of Korea are similar to those of China and Japan, two countries which have ruled Korea at various times in the past. Here, a Korean craftsman paints a bamboo design on an elegant vase.

The huge statue is of Buddha, who founded the Buddhist religion about 2,500 years ago. The people celebrate Buddha's birthday around the start of May. In Seoul, hundreds of thousands of people parade with lighted lanterns.

Buddhism was brought to Korea from China. South Korea has more than 700 Buddhist temples. Many are beautiful and contain large statues and paintings of Buddha. Buddhist monks wear long, flowing robes.

Music and dancing are popular arts. These musicians are followers of the ideas of Confucius, a great Chinese thinker, who lived at about the same time as Buddha. About five million Koreans are followers of Confucianism.

South Korea has more than 9 million Christians. Some 84 per cent of them are Protestants and 16 per cent are Roman Catholics. Missionaries from China introduced Christianity in the 17th century.

Like students in other parts of the world, young Koreans enjoy school outings to study the history and arts of their country. The Korean language is different from Chinese and Japanese and it has its own alphabet.

A Korean family enjoys a day out on a public holiday. Korean women used to marry young. Their husbands were chosen by match-makers. Today, however, most young people choose their own husbands or wives.

Many Koreans enjoy inviting their relations and friends to a traditional meal. They sit on the floor and eat from a low table. They use chopsticks instead of knives and forks and eat from small bowls.

The picture shows various Korean foods. A common dish, which most people eat daily, is called kimch'i. It is made of fermented radishes, Chinese cabbage or some other vegetable, with red spicy peppers and salt.

This modern resort is Haeund-dae Beach, east of the city of Pusan. Tourism is a growing industry. In the early 1980s, more than a million tourists went to Korea every year. Besides the sunny beaches, they visit the temples and historical sites.

Students relax outside Seoul University. Students are trained to play a part in increasing the country's wealth and living standards. Since the Korean War, South Korea has become one of eastern Asia's most prosperous countries.

Index